H

By United Library

https://campsite.bio/unitedlibrary

Table of Contents

Disclaimer

This biography book is a work of nonfiction based on the public life of a famous person. The author has used publicly available information to create this work. While the author has thoroughly researched the subject and attempted to depict it accurately, it is not meant to be an exhaustive study of the subject. The views expressed in this book are those of the author alone and do not necessarily reflect those of any organization associated with the subject. This book should not be taken as an endorsement, legal advice, or any other form of professional advice. This book was written for entertainment purposes only.

Introduction

The book Hedy Lamarr reveals the fascinating life of an American actress and inventor of Austro-Hungarian origin, who became a symbol of Hollywood's golden age. Born Hedwig Eva Maria Kiesler on November 9, 1914, Lamarr's career began with a brief film career in Czechoslovakia, marked by the controversial film "Extase" (1933). Fleeing her first husband, Fritz, a wealthy Austrian munitions manufacturer, Lamarr went underground in Paris before attracting the attention of Louis B. Mayer, head of the Metro-Goldwyn-Mayer studio in London.

Famous for her captivating performances in films such as "Algiers" (1938) and "Samson et Dalila" (1949), Lamarr rose to star status in Hollywood. The book explores her films at MGM, including "Lady of the Tropics" (1939), "Boom Town" (1940), "H. M. Pulham, Esq. (1941) and "White Cargo" (1942). Beyond her acting career, Lamarr's extraordinary contribution during the Second World War emerges, co-inventing a revolutionary radio guidance system for Allied torpedoes alongside avant-garde composer George Antheil. Their invention used spread spectrum and frequency hopping techniques to counter the radio jamming threats of the Axis powers.

This biography explores Lamarr's dual identity as Hollywood icon and innovative inventor, highlighting her enduring legacy in entertainment and technology.

Hedy Lamarr

Hedwig Kiesler, known as Hedy Lamarr, was an Austrian actress, film producer and inventor, naturalized American, born on November 9, 1914 in Vienna (then Austria-Hungary) and died on January 19, 2000 in Casselberry (Florida).

During her film career, she worked with some of the greatest directors, including King Vidor, Jack Conway, Victor Fleming, Jacques Tourneur, Marc Allégret, Cecil B. DeMille and Clarence Brown. A glamorous icon of American cinema, she was described in her day as "the most beautiful woman in cinema".

In addition to her film career, she left her mark on the scientific history of telecommunications by inventing, with composer George Antheil, a pianist and inventor like herself, a means of coding transmissions (frequency hopping spread spectrum). This is a fundamental transmission principle in telecommunications, used today for satellite positioning (GPS, etc.), encrypted military links and certain Wi-Fi techniques.

Biography

Youth

Born at the start of the Great War, Hedwig Eva Maria Kiesler, only daughter of Ashkenazi Jews from the Austro-Hungarian bourgeoisie, was too young to suffer the upheavals brought about by the defeat of 1918: the fall of the monarchy and the dismemberment of the Empire. She grew up in an Austria reduced to a small republic in the center of Europe.

His father Emil Kiesler (1880-1935), born in Lemberg (today Lviv, Ukraine), was director of the Creditanstalt-Bankverein bank in Vienna. His mother Gertrud Lichtwitz (1894-1977), from a large Jewish bourgeois family in Budapest, Hungary, was a concert pianist. She hoped to have a son named Georg. By adulthood, Gertrud had converted to Catholicism at the insistence of her first husband, and subsequently raised her daughter in this religion without having baptized her. Hedwig grew up in a privileged environment, having tutors and then attending a Swiss boarding school. In addition to German, Yiddish and Hungarian, she learned English and Italian, took dance and piano lessons, went horseback riding and attended the opera.

At the age of 12, Hedwig Kiesler won a beauty contest in Vienna. She was already interested in theater and film, but after a "revelation" when she saw Fritz Lang's *Metropolis* (1927), she wanted to become an actress. Her father explained the workings of certain technologies to her on walks, and at home she often did odd jobs.

Careers in Europe

At the age of 16, Hedwig Kiesler presented herself to the Sascha Studios in Vienna, probably recommended by a relative of her parents, whose financial situation had deteriorated with the Austrian economic crisis of the 1930s. The future Hedy Lamarr entered "the world of expressive silence" through her compatriot director Georg Jacoby. Jacoby hired her for two films - *Geld auf der Strasse* with Rosa Albach-Retty and *Tempête dans un verre d'eau*, in 1930 and 1931 - and then as a script girl to keep her close to him.

A school dropout, she was hired by theater director Max Reinhardt, who presented her to the press as "the most beautiful girl in the world"; it was at this time that she met Otto Preminger and Sam Spiegel, who vied for her favors, and whom she later met again among the Jews who had emigrated like her to the United States.

Hedwig Kiesler moved to Berlin in 1931, where she made Alexis Granowsky's *Les Treize Malles de monsieur O. F.,* starring Peter Lorre and Margo Lion - a film for which Hedwig was the subject of a noisy publicity campaign, with interesting repercussions, since even the *New York Times* praised her presence - and then in 1932 *Pas besoin d'argent*, by the pro-Nazi Carl Boese (co-director of the classic *The Golem*), which was a great success.

At the same time, she played one of the four main characters in Noël Coward's *Private Lives* (*Les Amants terribles), a* performance that earned her rave reviews.

As she sits reading a script, filmmaker Gustav Machatý notices her beauty and gives her a few bad films, followed in 1933 by *Extase*, a Czechoslovakian film with virtually no dialogue but a sophisticated aesthetic. The screenplay was similar to that of *Lady Chatterley's Lover;* the film caused a worldwide sensation and made the actress famous. She says she naively carried out the instructions for the nude scene and the first on-screen orgasm scene, in which we see only her face. She makes no moral judgment on the heroine's conduct. She acquired a sultry reputation at the age of 19 that would never leave her, and much of Europe already dubbed her "*The Ecstasy Girl*". Even though the first censors had demanded that a marriage be inserted into the film before the actress' ecstasy could take place, the film, presented at the Venice Biennale, was condemned by Pope Pius XII; Hitler, newly in power, banned it in Germany, and the controversial scenes were expunged from most European and American versions.

Hedwig Kiesler also enjoyed great success on stage as Elisabeth of Austria (Sissi).

Friedrich Mandl, an arms manufacturer and supplier to Mussolini, noticed the young actress in *Extase*, and their relationship led to a marriage of convenience in 1933: the husband had, in all likelihood, also been encouraged by his future in-laws, who were worried about the future of their offspring. But the freedom-loving young woman, too closely watched by her husband - who forbade her to continue acting and tried to buy back all copies of the film *Extase* - fled her gilded life in 1937. She went to Switzerland, where she rubbed shoulders with the jet set, but also with the Austrian-Jewish émigré like herself, Billy Wilder, Kay Francis, the Paramount star and the German writer Erich Maria Remarque, who owned a superb villa in Porto Ronco on Lake Maggiore, where he offered asylum to those fleeing Nazi Germany: she began an affair with him that kept her off the screen for another year.

Through the American agent Bob Ritchie, she met Louis B. Mayer in London, who was looking for European talent. Mayer in London, who was looking for European talent. Apparently uninterested in Hedwig Kiesler, embarrassed in particular by her performance in *Extase* (according to her), Mayer, the Hollywood magnate, offered her an unattractive contract (six-month trial and one hundred and fifty dollars a week), which she refused. According to Mayer, she was housekeeper to the violin prodigy Grisha Goluboff, with whom she boarded the *Normandie* to cross the Atlantic. On board, where Mayer and Cole Porter were also present - the latter would later write a song about her - Hedwig put on her best face to impress Mayer, convincing him to hire her on her terms (five hundred dollars a week). However, the film mogul, who had stuck to the sultry image of the film that had made his name, never held her in high esteem, going so far as to avoid saying hello to her when he saw her.

Career in the United States

The MGM star

Hedwig Kiesler reappears on the screen, linked to Metro-Goldwyn-Mayer (MGM) by a seven-year contract, during which she plays in some fifteen feature films. Her American career began with John Cromwell's *Casbah* (1938), produced by Walter Wanger and United Artists, a remake of Julien Duvivier's *Pépé le Moko*, in which she took on the role of Mireille Balin, and Charles Boyer that of Jean Gabin.

As soon as she arrived in Hollywood, she changed her name to Hedy Lamarr, on the suggestion of MGM publicist Howard Strickland; "Hedy" is a diminutive of her first name Hedwig, and "Lamarr" is said to have originated from her "sea" cruise aboard the *Normandie* with Mayer. Other sources suggest that it was a tribute suggested by Mayer to the actress Barbara La Marr, who precociously died in 1926.

After the Anschluss in March 1938, Hedy Lamarr brought her mother to the United States, where she later obtained American citizenship. She indicated "Hebrew" under "race" on the naturalization form, a term then frequently used in Europe.

Considered Hollywood's revelation of the moment, she continued in the exotic vein with Jack Conway's romance *The Lady of the Tropics*, from a screenplay by Ben Hecht, with Robert Taylor as her partner, and, alongside Spencer Tracy, began the complex filming of *This Woman is Mine*, also from a screenplay by Hecht, begun by Josef von Sternberg, taken up by the uncredited Frank Borzage and completed by W. S. Van Dyke, nicknamed "One Shot Woody", who signed it alone.

After a successful debut and a disappointing career, her performances were sometimes poorly received by the critics. Luther Green asked her to play *Salomé* on stage, but the studio objected.

She made a name for herself in King Vidor's anti-Soviet comedy *Comrade X*, opposite Clark Gable, again with a screenplay by Ben Hecht: in a role similar to *Ninotchka* filmed the previous year, she parodied Greta Garbo by deepening her voice and, if she intervened late in the film, amused audiences with incongruous situations such as the one in which she drove a streetcar filled with goats and peasants in frock coats. The parodic vein once again won her critical and public acclaim.

She reunites with Spencer Tracy and Jack Conway in the adventures of *Oil Fever,* in a role that heralds the future heroines of his films noirs*, and with* King Vidor in the nostalgic *Souvenirs* with Robert Young, which denounces an oppressive Puritan order.

Along with Judy Garland and Lana Turner, Lamarr appeared in Robert Z. Leonard's *La Danseuse des Folies Ziegfeld.* Leonard, one of the big hits of 1941.

Clarence Brown employed her in the romantic *Viens avec moi*, and Victor Fleming directed her with John Garfield and Spencer Tracy in the adaptation of John Steinbeck's realistic novel *Tortilla Flat*, about the lives of poor Californian fishermen; critic Pauline Kael praised Hedy Lamarr. At the same time, Conway directs her for the third time, along with William Powell, in the melodrama *Crossroads*.

In Richard Thorpe's *Tondelayo,* dressed in black, the actress plays a native of Sierra Leone on the African continent, the vile temptress of Walter Pidgeon and Richard Carlson. Actor and biographer Stephen Michael Shearer calls her role "a teasing exercise in 1940s eroticism at its most vulgar".

She made another comedy, Alexander Hall's *Heavenly Body*, which gave her Powell back as her partner, an astronomer husband who proclaimed like a slogan: "It's heaven to be in love with Hedy".

During the Second World War, as an exiled anti-fascist, she participated in the American war effort, alongside Paul Henreid, Sydney Greenstreet and Peter Lorre, with Jean Negulesco's film noir *Les Conspirateurs* (1944), a contemporary spy story inspired by the success of *Casablanca*. She sells $25 million worth of war bonds, visiting numerous American cities and promoting letters of support for the G.I.'s.

In a similar vein, in Jacques Tourneur's *Angoisse*, she plays a thriller heroine, somewhere between Irish George Brent and Austro-Hungarian Paul Lukas. The film was RKO's most expensive production of 1944; Hedy Lamarr insisted that the contemporary action of Margaret Seymour Carpenter's (en) novel be transposed to the turn of the century, with a reconstruction of 1903 New York; as the action took place in the cosmopolitan upper middle class of the East Coast, the interior sets, costumes and photography were equally luxurious.

In 1945, she starred in the last film of her MGM contract, the Richard Thorpe-directed comedy *The Princess and the Bellboy*, co-starring Robert Walker. Mayer's ambitions fizzled out. From Sternberg to Thorpe, Hedy Lamarr failed to become the new Garbo.

Femme fatale and glamour queen roles

From *Casbah* onwards and in all her MGM films, Hedy Lamarr played a glamorous queen, as was common at the time with Joan Crawford, whose appeal was fading, or Greta Garbo, already retired.

Her physique as "*The Queen of Glamour*" is detailed by the press: her "jet hair", her "marbled blue-green" or "chameleon blue" eyes, "perfectly symmetrical", her "fine, straight nose", her "porcelain skin", her "mouth comparable to the flight of a bird", her "dreamy little smile and her voice with an exotic accent", a combination of Viennese accent and MGM diction school.

Actresses like Joan Bennett (whose ex-husband Gene Markey she later married) dyed their hair black, parting it in the middle, and waving it in vague curls to resemble Lamarr, who had been called "the most beautiful woman in cinema".

Triumph and decline

In 1946, Hedy Lamarr moved into independent production. *The Demon of the Flesh* was partly directed by Douglas Sirk, another Berlin emigre, and signed by Viennese Edgar Ulmer, expressly chosen by Hedy Lamarr. Set in New England at the beginning of the 19th century, this exaggeratedly romantic costume psychodrama offered the actress her best role: the portrait of a schizophrenic criminal. Based on a novel by Ben Ames Williams (also the author of *Deadly Sin*, whose screen adaptation earned Gene Tierney an Oscar nomination), Lamarr co-stars with George Sanders and Louis Hayward. Along with *Extase* and *Samson et Dalila,* this film remains one of his classics.

The failure of her next film, Robert Stevenson's *The Dishonored Wife,* starring John Loder (whom she married), marked the abrupt end of her activity as a producer in 1947.

The following nine years were marked by relative discretion, despite the triumph of Cecil B. DeMille's peplum *Samson et Dalila* (1949), inspired by the *Book of Judges* and starring Victor Mature, George Sanders and Angela Lansbury, in which, in one scene, she received a fortune in emeralds and sapphires to match the color of her eyes; the film established her image as a cold, heartless femme fatale for a long time to come. In August of the same year, she made the cover of *Paris Match*.

The actress moved on from Richard Wallace's comedy *Let's Live a Little* (1948), starring Robert Cummings and the Russian Anna Sten, to Joseph H. Lewis's spy film *The Lady Without a Passport*, set in Havana under Batista. Comedy and espionage came together in Norman Z. McLeod's *Espionne de mon cœur* (1951). McLeod, alongside Bob Hope. She also experimented with westerns (with little success) at Paramount, in John Farrow's *Terre Damnée* (1950), as a saloon owner opposite Ray Milland.

She rounded off her career in Marc Allégret's *L'amante di Paride* (1954), where she played the mythical Helen of Troy and Empress Josephine, and in the documentary *L'Histoire de l'humanité*, directed and produced by Irwin Allen, also starring Ronald Colman and the Marx Brothers, in which she played Joan of Arc.

In 1958, the actress shared the credits of her last official film, Harry Keller's *Femmes devant le désir (en)* (*The Female Animal*), with soprano Jane Powell: "quite an absorbing study of the world of actresses", according to Gérard Legrand. At the end of March, she is the surprise guest on the popular CBS entertainment show *What's My Line?* The same year sees the death of Mayer, her second "father in cinema" after Jacoby.

In the wake of her greatest success, *Samson et Dalila*, the star's fall from grace began. Hedy Lamarr retired in 1957 after a series of failures. Her fame had already faded; her last appearance in volume 26 of *Who's Who in America* dates from 1950-1951.

In 1960, she was honored with a star on the *Hollywood Walk of Fame*.

According to obscure sources, she led a social life for a few years and squandered her fortune. In the 1960s, she was arrested several times for shoplifting beauty products. She moved from California to an apartment on New York's East Side, the better to handle her various lawsuits, notably against the publisher of her book *Ecstasy and Me*, over the rights to an unreleased Italian film in which she had starred, against her ex-husband Howard Lee, who allegedly had her co-sign his loans, and in her defense against charges of kleptomania.

The arrest after her first robbery at the May Company department store, the publicity surrounding it and her subsequent stay for overwork in a Los Angeles rest hospital prompted producer Joseph E. Levine, with whom she had just begun working in 1965 on a horror film entitled (en)*Picture Mommy Dead*, to claim that she had deserted the picture, and fired her, thus ending her Hollywood career.

Plagued by the fear of aging, she takes great care of herself, then experiments with cosmetic surgery, to no avail.

End of life

His mother, Gertrud Kiesler, died in 1977, far from her husband, who had been buried in Vienna in 1935, and was buried in California.

In the last decades of her life, Hedy Lamarr communicated only by telephone with the outside world, even with her children and close friends, living as a recluse in her Florida apartment. She often talked for up to six or seven hours a day on the phone, but spent virtually no time with anyone in person.

A documentary film, *Calling Hedy Lamarr*, released in 2004, features her children, Anthony Loder and Denise Loder-DeLuca.

Death

Hedy Lamarr died on January 19, 2000 at the age of 85 in Casselberry, Florida, after suffering from heart disease. In accordance with her wishes, her remains were cremated and, in 2014, her son Anthony Loder spread some of her ashes in the Austrian woods around Vienna.

In the documentary *Calling Hedy Lamarr*, co-directed by the actress's son Anthony Loder, we see him throw half of his mother's ashes into the woods surrounding Vienna, the city of her childhood to which she never returned. We also see him noting the omission of Hedy Lamarr from the Walk of Fame, where his mother was awarded the star number 6,247.

Since November 7, 2014, the urn containing the other half of Lamarr's ashes has rested, according to Anthony Loder's wishes, in Vienna's Central Cemetery, shortly before his mother's 100th birthday.

Scientific and technical activities

Hedy Lamarr had interests other than acting: she was a keen designer and talented inventor (she claimed that ideas came naturally to her). Until her death, she never stopped producing inventions, leaving behind her many ingenious projects. One invention she co-authored was patented in 1941.

Conversations with her friend, the avant-garde composer George Antheil, an anti-Nazi and anti-fascist like herself, gave rise to the idea of an invention she believed would put an end to the torpedoing of passenger liners. It was a signal transmission principle known as *frequency-hopping spread* spectrum (FHSS).

This principle of frequency hopping spread spectrum transmission is still used in the 21st century for satellite positioning (GPS, GLONASS...), military encrypted links, space shuttle communications with the ground, mobile telephony and Wi-Fi technology. However, this principle differs from Direct Sequence Spread Spectrum (DSSS), used in certain Wi-Fi standards, such as IEEE 802.11b.

Lamarr became acquainted with various weapons technologies, including torpedo control systems, when she was married (from 1933 to 1937) to Friedrich Mandl, a major Austrian munitions manufacturer who traded with the Austrian Heimwehr and supplied Mussolini.

George Antheil, for his part, is familiar with automatic control systems and frequency hopping sequences, which he uses in his musical compositions and performances, based on the principle of perforated piano rolls (*pianola*).

To help the Allies in their war effort, in December 1940 both proposed their invention to the National Inventors Council, an association of inventors in the field, and on June 10, 1941 decided to patent their "secret communication *system*", applicable to radio-controlled torpedoes, to enable the torpedo's transceiver system to change frequency, making it virtually impossible for the enemy to detect an underwater attack. The invention is immediately made available free of charge to the U.S. Army.

The U.S. Patent Office holds the description of a secret communication system for radio-guided devices, applied to torpedoes for example, with co-authors George Antheil and Hedy Lamarr (under the name "Hedy Kiesler Markey", an error mixing her stage name with her real surname, aged 27 at the time). U.S. Patent No. 2 292 387 (filed June 10, 1941, registered August 11, 1942) describes a system for simultaneously varying transmitter and receiver frequencies, according to the same registered code (the medium used being perforated tapes inspired by player piano cards), where Antheil gives full credit for the functional part to Lamarr, specifying that his work on the patent was merely technical. The patent has recently been dubbed the "Lamarr technique".

However, this idea was so innovative that the U.S. Navy didn't immediately grasp its importance, finding it "impractical"; it was therefore not put into practice at the time, although in the 1950s there was a project for submarine detection by aircraft using this technique. Hedy Lamarr does not mention this invention, or the patent application, in her sulphurous memoirs. Later, advances in electronics meant that the process was used - officially for the first time by the US Army - during the Cuban missile crisis in 1962 and during the Vietnam War.

When the patent fell into the public domain in 1959, the device was also used by manufacturers of transmission equipment, particularly since the 1980s. Most cell phones take advantage of the principles of Lamarr and Antheil's invention.

Recognition

In 1973, the founders of the first "National Inventor's Day" published a press release with the names of unexpected inventors, including Hedy Lamarr, the woman who had made missiles stealthier. Lamarr, then aged 59, was surprised, unaware until then that her patent had been used; and decided to obtain rights in vain. But she never received any financial compensation for her invention (estimated to be worth 30 billion dollars) despite her claims, unaware that US law allowed only six years after patent filing to claim it, and often still hearing the reply that her invention had not been used.

In 1997, Hedy Lamarr received the Electronic Frontier Foundation Award for her contribution to society. Living in seclusion in Florida at the age of 82, she did not attend the ceremony for fear that people would make fun of her appearance. An accusation of espionage and plagiarism by Robert Price, a historian specializing in secret communications, contributed to her invention being forgotten in the collective memory. Film historian Jeanine Basinger (en) believes that in another era, Lamarr "could very well have become a scientist. It's an option that has suffered from her great beauty".

Hedy Lamarr offsets her bitterness against the movie moguls: "They wanted something cheap and stupid," she says, "they wanted something stupid but I have little shelves in my brain".

From the 2000s onwards, she became a symbol of innovation and design; her genius was celebrated. In

2003, she appeared on the front cover of *Dignifying Science: Stories About Women Scientists*. *Science & Vie* and *Guerres & Histoire* dubbed her the "*Brain Bomb*". An Austrian invention prize bears her name, and her birthday, November 9, marks Inventor's Day in German-speaking countries.

In 2014, the "most beautiful woman in cinema" turned "homing bomb" and pianist George Antheil were posthumously inducted into the National Inventors Hall of Fame.

Privacy policy

The seductress

Hedy Lamarr is one of Hollywood's great seductresses.

In an article from *Ciné Télé Revue* in July 1950, Hedy Lamarr is described as follows:

"The first thing she notices when one of these handsome gentlemen is introduced to her is his walk, his manner. Is he friendly, courteous, distinguished? Does he look fresh and well-groomed? Hedy hates men who look as if they've forgotten to shave, as well as all those who take a malicious pleasure in putting their hands deep in their pockets and their feet up on the desk."

Hedy Lamarr's 1966 memoir *Ecstasy and Me* damaged her image as an untouchable goddess. In France, two years later, it was the subject of a review by Bernard Cohn in *Positif*. In it, the star dwells on her eventful and particularly sexual private life. According to *Playboy*, this memoir is one of the ten most erotic autobiographies of all time, alongside *The Sexual Life of Catherine M.*, *The Memoirs of Casanova* and the autobiographies of Klaus Kinski and Motley Crue.

Lamarr believed that the book's frankness had put an end to his career and blamed his pen-pushers, but the court ruled against Lamarr on the grounds that his persistent image of low morality, invoked in the book's title described as "dirty, nauseating and revolting", made it very easy to believe that its contents were not libel but truth. The book was even preceded by two introductions, one medical and one psychiatric, as sexual activity outside marriage was then considered pathological.

Hedy Lamarr collects adventures. In England, she seduced Stewart Granger, still married to actress Elspeth March (en). She calls him "one of the loveliest men in the world".

In March 1941, billionaire Howard Hughes showered her with gifts. In August 1942, she dated Jean-Pierre Aumont, then Mark Stevens in September, and her engagement to George Montgomery was broken off in November, according to *The Hollywood Reporter*.

In *Ecstasy and Me*, she recounts how, in 1945, John Kennedy, who was visiting Paris, phoned to ask her to come and asked what she wanted; she replied "oranges". She invited him to her apartment, where he arrived an hour later with a bag of oranges; citrus fruit being virtually impossible to find at the time, the gift was much appreciated.

Among the various personalities with whom the star is said to have been in close contact:

- Sam Spiegel (producer of *Sur les quais* and *Le Pont de la rivière Kwaï*), met in Berlin;

- Johnny Carson, host of The *Tonight Show*;

- photographer Robert Capa;

- director Frank Borzage, who directed her on *I Take this Woman*;

- actors David Niven, Errol Flynn, Marlon Brando ;

- actors and directors Orson Welles and Charlie Chaplin, Billy Wilder and Otto Preminger, two Viennese directors she met in Europe before the war, her partners Charles Boyer, Clark Gable (she denied it), George Sanders, James Stewart, John Garfield, Robert Taylor, Robert Walker, Spencer Tracy, Ray Milland.

Once sharing her "sex addiction", which at the time might have seemed out of place, she concluded, "It's a curse for a woman to have too many needs."

Weddings

Hedy Lamarr made a name for herself through six marriages, the first of which, when she was 19, proved to be the most famous: Friedrich Mandl was one of the world's four biggest arms dealers, a personal friend and supplier to Mussolini, a Jew who converted to Catholicism to trade with the Austrian Heimwehr and was promoted to "honorary Aryan" by Josef Goebbels. By 1933, he had made her an institution of Vienna's high society, receiving foreign leaders including Hitler, according to Lamarr's memoirs, and Hermann Goering. Her task was to look pretty, sport jewels and furs, and speak or laugh very little: "He always treated me like a doll," she reports, "I had to spend all my time giving and going to parties, wearing elegant clothes, taking pleasure trips to Switzerland, North Africa, the Côte d'Azur..." Mandl tried, according to an unlikely but supported legend, to buy back all the posters in which she appears languishing and the copies of the film *Extase,* only to destroy them. Moreover, Lamarr left her because he was too involved with the Nazis and his sick jealousy was suffocating her in the gilded cage in which he confined her. According to the same legend, she escaped after drugging the maid in charge of watching her, borrowing her uniform.

Of her subsequent husbands, we may note: with screenwriter and producer Gene Markey (en) (1939-1940), whom Hedy Lamarr later declared "was the only civilized man: he spat into a spittoon", she adopted little James Markey Lamarr, whom, after a custody battle, she soon dismissed from her life, and who, in 1969, turned out to be the main protagonist of a news item (having become a policeman, he killed a 14-year-old black boy). With actor John Loder (1943-1947), she had two children, Anthony and Denise, with whom she had a difficult relationship, despite some fine declarations, as the actress had a heavy hand (Denise told of crying while playing with a doll bearing the effigy of her often-absent mother). Next in line were actor and Acapulco real estate tycoon Teddy Stauffer (en) (1951-1952), Texas oil industrialist W. Howard Lee (1953-1960) and her previous divorce lawyer Lewis J. Boies (1963-1965). Her longest marriage, to Howard Lee, was confirmed by the actress's own admission as a "black page" in her life; she was in litigation against him for a long time.

Hedy Lamarr married and divorced six times:

- Friedrich Mandl, Austrian arms manufacturer (1933-1937)

- Gene Markey (en) (1939-1940); a son (adopted), James

- John Loder (1943-1947); two children, Denise and Anthony

- Teddy Stauffer (1951-1952)

- W. Howard Lee (1953-1960)

- Lewis J. Boies (1963-1965).

Her various unions make her say: "I have to stop marrying men who feel inferior to me. Somewhere there must be a man who could be my husband and not feel inferior. I need a man who is both superior and inferior.

Children

Hedy Lamarr had three children:

- James Loder (born March 6, 1939), child adopted with her husband Gene Markey, and adopted by her husband John Loder on October 16, 1939 as James Markey Lamarr.

- Denise Hedy Loder (born May 29, 1945)

- Anthony Loder (born March 1, 1947)

Judaism

Her Jewishness is an element of her biography that she never mentions in her autobiography, in interviews or even to her children.

Subversion and nudity

Hedy Lamarr is one of the most famous actresses to have appeared fully nude on film, in the Czech film *Extase* (1933), which predates her Hollywood career. According to her, she was guaranteed to be filmed from afar.

In *Grandes Dames du cinéma* (1993), Don Macpherson laments Lamarr's lack of "that distinct charm and personality that would echo her beauty"; he hails "one of her most delightful professional efforts" in *La Danseuse des Folies Ziegfeld*, and hits the nail on the head in Cecil B. DeMille's hit peplum Samson et Dalila (1949). DeMille's successful peplum (*Samson et Dalila*, 1949): "Lamarr embodies Dalila with a beneficent disregard for realism", alongside Victor Mature "whose acting prowess is in the same vein".

The author acknowledges, however, that "her determination and panache" help to save the film, and concludes on this note: "Amidst the ruins of her 'technicolored' temple, doesn't it seem that she has finally found her place, however fleeting her glory".

As for *Casablanca,* Hedy Lamarr was contacted, as were Irene Dunne and Michèle Morgan (too expensive), but she was under contract to MGM and didn't want to commit to a project without knowing the script - nor did the crew, including Bogart and Bergman, appreciate the improvised nature of the shoot.

Rumor also has it that many well-known actresses turned Bogart down because they didn't find him attractive enough. In 1942, Bogart had only two starring roles to his credit, in *The Great Escape* and *The Maltese Falcon*.

Ingrid Bergman, meanwhile, was just starting out in the U.S., where she had only made the remake of *Intermezzo* and *Doctor Jekyll and Mr. Hyde*. Even Jack Warner couldn't believe how sexy Bogart looked, and he himself credited his partner. On the other hand, George Cukor, director of *Haunting, couldn't* remember Hedy Lamarr ever being mentioned in that project.

In the *Larousse* article, the film critic deplores the fact that "MGM's sanitized aesthetic" accentuated the "natural coldness of her acting", and measures the actress's abilities against her performance in *The Flesh Demon*. As for Mayer, the book insists on her conception of the star: "elegant, diaphanous, distant" and underlines the general mawkishness of MGM films after the death of Irving Thalberg (1936). For Jean Tulard, his career included "no great masterpieces, but some excellent strips".

The woman hasn't received better reviews than the performer. From the point of view of French actor Jean-Pierre Aumont :

"At a dinner party to which Hedy Lamarr had invited him, the actor suddenly felt his hostess's leg rubbing against his under the table... Eight days later, Hedy and Jean-Pierre were engaged. After giving a solitaire to the lady of his heart, the actor phoned his father to ask him to come to Los Angeles to meet his future daughter-in-law. By the time Mr. Aumont Sr. made the trip, Jean-Pierre had realized that he was about to make a mistake: capricious, vain, Hedy was definitely not the woman for him. Welcoming his father at the airport, Jean-Pierre told him of his decision to break up with Hedy and entrusted him with the task of notifying his fiancée. The news was not well received. When she saw the actor again, Hedy threw her ring in his face, then, changing her mind, picked it up and slammed the door!"

With Howard Lee, love turns to hate. Gene Tierney recalls, in her autobiography *Mademoiselle, vous devriez faire du cinéma*:

"Howard Lee was in the middle of divorce proceedings with Hedy Lamarr. Long before the tourists came to town, he had built a house called Villa of Aspen (formerly Villa Lamarr). (...) At the mere mention of my name, he spat: 'No way! I've had my fill of movie actresses!" (...) If he believed, or dreaded, a Hollywood creature, I no longer fit that category, insofar as that was ever the case."

Jane Powell, talking about Hedy Lamarr's last official film, *Femmes devant le désir (en)* (*The Female Animal*, 1958), recounts:

"Hedy Lamarr was obsessed by her age and beauty. She couldn't stand being the mother of a grown woman and had forbidden any scenes with me, which was totally unreasonable since I was supposed to be her daughter. She was a star through and through. Every day she would arrive at the studio in a limousine driven by her chauffeur and rush to the make-up room along a red carpet that had been carefully rolled out for her. One day, she slammed the door in the face of the entire team, believing that a joke we were laughing at concerned her."

The black legend

According to pianist and composer George Antheil, "Hedy was an intellectual giant compared to other Hollywood actresses". Appearances often did her a disservice, and loneliness and melancholy seemed to attach themselves to her. Her unsuccessful plastic surgery and a few sordid incidents, contradictory rumors, make up her "black legend".

In François Truffaut's film *La Nuit américaine*, during a crisis of despair that the cast and crew can't explain, lead actress Julie Bake (played by Jacqueline Bisset) demands butter in a lump. A simple observer, one of the lead actors (played by Jean-Pierre Aumont, who had been engaged to Lamarr), comments:

" ... He [the director] is still lucky in his misfortune. I've known far more expensive whims. There was an Austrian actress, Hedy Lamarr, who was one of Hollywood's queens; she missed the rainy climate of her native Tyrol so much that she had a rainmaking machine installed in the garden of her California estate. So you see, butter in a lump... "

- Jean-Pierre Aumont's dialogue in *La Nuit américaine*.

In 1949, Hedy Lamarr won the only award of her career, the Golden Apple Award for Least Cooperative Actress. This misanthropy was not confined to journalists: the July 18-24, 1950 issue of *Ciné Télé Revue* reported:

"Hedy Lamarr no longer likes to be talked about. She hates interviews and distrusts the sincerity of her friends. She doesn't have many friends any more. She's had too many disappointments and dreads them. She's almost a recluse. Above all, don't ask her too specific questions: let her speak from her heart. When she's feeling down, as she is now, it's her Viennese childhood she thinks about most intensely, and her father. And of her father.

His life was marked by female friendships, such as his childhood friendship with the great Viennese singer Greta Keller: admired by the Prince of Wales and King Carol of Romania, she debuted with Peter Lorre and Marlene Dietrich and became the first star of the Oak Room (en) cabaret.

In 1939, Lamarr's fans included actresses Katharine Hepburn and Greta Garbo, Tallulah Bankhead and actor Clifton Webb. Another of her friends, Ann Sothern, was the comic heroine of the *Maisie* series and one of the performers in Joseph Mankiewicz's *Conjugal Chains* (1949).

In 1960, Lamarr was arrested for shoplifting and released without trial. In 1966, caught shoplifting beauty products from a Los Angeles department store, she was tried and acquitted on the grounds of a misunderstanding. It was a defeated Hedy Lamarr who explained herself in front of the cameras. In Ava Gardner's memoirs, actress Lena Horne recounts:

"When I met Hedy Lamarr after one of my shows, she said, "MGM was wonderful! They picked out our clothes, we didn't have to think about anything, Howard Strickling (en) took care of everything and anticipated what we'd have to say." And this remark had a strange effect on me, because I knew there was something horrible going on. You always need to be able to think for yourself."

In the mid-1960s, Andy Warhol made the acquaintance of Hedy Lamarr, whose memoirs inspired the 1965 parodic melodrama *Hedy (The Most Beautiful Woman in the World/The Shoplifter/The Fourteen Year Old Girl),* which recounts the end of a woman's life and the myth of immortality as she fights time with surgery, "ridiculing her post-film career". In this film, after shoplifting, the heroine (played by transvestite Mario Montez (en)) undergoes a tough interrogation by an investigator.

In 1990, *Télé Poche* magazine mentioned a Lamarr biographical TV movie starring Melissa Morgan, a former skater and actress in *Les Feux de l'amour*.

The following year, Jean Tulard wrote that she had "sunk into anonymity and, it is said, misery". The same year, Hedy Lamarr re-offended at the Eckerd supermarket in Casselberry, Florida, where she lived: she was sentenced to one year's probation.

Author and star confidante Joan MacTrevor confirmed Lamarr's ease in 1990:

"Born [...] of a Hungarian mother known worldwide for her beauty and a bank manager father, she is rich. She even owns an island in the Caribbean. As she recently told the press: "A woman must take care of herself until her last breath. She can't let her looks and beauty deteriorate!" [...] Hedy Lamarr probably couldn't bear to be forgotten by her fans. Now suffering from cataracts, she gives the sad image of a fallen star."

Filmography

Cinema

- 1930: *Geld auf der Straße* by Georg Jacoby: the girl at the nightclub table

- 1931: *Tempête dans un verre d'eau* (*Die Blumenfrau von Lindenau*) by Georg Jacoby: the secretary

- 1931: *Les Treize Malles de monsieur O. F.* by Alexis Granowsky: Hélène, the mayor's daughter

- 1932: *Man braucht kein Geld* by Carl Boese: Käthe Brandt

- 1933: *Extase* by Gustav Machatý: Éva Hermann

- 1938: *Casbah* by John Cromwell: Gaby

- 1939: *The Lady of the Tropics* by Jack Conway: Manon deVargnes Carey / Kira Kim

- 1940: *This Woman is Mine* by W.S. Van Dyke: Georgi Gragore Decker

- 1940: *Oil Fever* by Jack Conway: Karen Vanmeer

- 1940: *Comrade X* by King Vidor: Golubka, or Theodore Yahupitz and Lizvanetchka "Lizzie".

- 1941: *Come with me* by Clarence Brown: Johnny Jones

- 1941: *La Danseuse des Folies Ziegfeld* by Robert Z. Leonard: Mrs. Sandra Kolter

- 1941: King Vidor's *Souvenirs*: Marvin Myles Ransome

- 1942: *Tortilla Flat* by Victor Fleming: Dolores Ramirez

- 1942: *Crossroads* by Jack Conway: Lucienne Talbot

- 1942: *Tondelayo* by Richard Thorpe: Tondelayo

- 1944: Alexander Hall's *Heavenly Body*: Vicky Whitley

- 1944: Jean Negulesco's *Les Conspirateurs*: Irène Von Mohr

- 1944: *Angoisse* by Jacques Tourneur: Allida Bederaux

- 1945: *The Princess and the Bellboy* by Richard Thorpe: Princess Veronica

- 1946: *The Flesh Demon* by Edgar G. Ulmer: Jenny Hager

- 1947: *La Femme déshonorée* by Robert Stevenson: Madeleine Damien

- 1948: *Let's Live a Little* by Richard Wallace: Dr. J.O. Loring

- 1949: *Samson and Delilah* by Cecil B. DeMille: Delilah

- 1950: *The Lady without a Passport* by Joseph H. Lewis: Marianne Lorress

- 1950: *Damned Earth* by John Farrow: Lisa Roselle

- 1951: *Spy of my heart* by Norman Z. McLeod: Lily Dalbray

- 1954: *L'Amante di Paride* by Marc Allégret and Edgar G. Ulmer: Hedy Windsor / Hélène de Troie / Empress Joséphine de Beauharnais / Geneviève de Brabant

- 1954: *L'Eterna femmina* by Marc Allégret

- 1957: *The History of Mankind* by Irwin Allen: Joan of Arc

- 1958: *Femmes devant le désir (en)* (*The Female Animal*) by Harry Keller: Vanessa Windsor

Television

- 1952: *Four Star Revue* (series): guest star
- 1957: *Zane Grey Theater* (series): Consuela Bowers

Producer

- 1946: *The Flesh Demon* by Edgar George Ulmer

Tributes

"Let's Speak of Lamarr, that Edy so fair,
Why does she let Joan Bennett wear all her old hair?"

- Cole Porter, *Let's No Talk About Love*, 1941.

The song is cruel to Joan Bennett, who was then making a career as a brunette femme fatale with Fritz Lang and Jean Renoir, having been a young blonde leading lady, married to Walter Wanger (the producer of *Casbah*) and ex-wife of Gene Markey (Hedy's second husband)... Apparently, the song was inspired by Lamarr's first Hollywood appearance, which made a strong impression, so Joan Bennet decided to go brunette like many women at the time.

"Sir Henry - You see the little house at the end of the road, opposite the one where Monsieur Poirot stayed last year? Well, it's been rented by a film star. The neighbors are gobsmacked.
 Midge - Is she really as fascinating as they say?
 Sir Henry - Well, I haven't seen her yet, but I understand she's around these days... What's her name again?
 Midge - Hedy Lamarr?"

- Agatha Christie, *The Valley*, 1946

"I think Hedy to be one of the most underestimated actresses, one who has not been lucky enough to get the most desirable roles. I have seen her do a few brilliant things. I always thought she had great talent, and as far as classical beauty is concerned you could not then, nor perhaps even now, find anyone to top Lamarr."

- Errol Flynn, *My Wicked Wicked Ways*, 1959.

Flynn also wanted to cast Hedy Lamarr in the female lead in *William Tell* (1943/1944), one of his most cherished projects, which never saw the light of day.

"When I first met Hedy Lamarr some twenty years ago, she was so breathtaking that all conversation stopped as soon as she entered a room. Wherever she went, she became the center of attention. I doubt anyone cared if there was anything behind this beauty. Everyone was too busy staring at her with their mouths agape."

- George Sanders, *Mémoires d'une fripouille*, 1960 (PUF reprint, p. 155)

"But talk about an entrance! Hedy Lamarr holds the record for that. One entrance she made at Ciro's is a vision I'll never forget.
Hedy was at the height of her beauty, with thick, wavy, jet-black hair. With that stunning widow's peak, her face was magnificent. We all looked up and there she was at the top of the stairs. She wore a cape of some kind up to

her chin, and it swept down to the floor. I can't even remember the color of the cape, because all I saw was that incredible face, that magnificent hair... She was enough to make strong men faint."

- Lana Turner, *Lana, the Lady, the Legend, the Truth*, 1982

"She had incredible, wonderful skin, with an unimaginable luminosity... Meeting her gave me one of the greatest thrills of my life. I was twenty-five, *The Nude and the Dead had just* been published and I was in Hollywood, where a party was being given, more or less in my honor. And Hedy Lamarr was there. I was flabbergasted, terribly enthusiastic. But, of course, I pretended to be completely blasé. She asked me if I was married. I replied, "Yes, I've fallen into the trap too." She looked at me and said, "You're a young scatterbrain, you shouldn't talk about marriage in those terms." For someone who's been divorced six times... I still think she was the most beautiful woman I've ever seen."

- Norman Mailer (1987).

"You didn't miss that beautiful face of hers. Oh, it was fabulous, just fabulous! People assume,apparently because of her beauty, that Hedy is a blank. Not at all. She was always charming when I knew her, with a nice sense of humor. "

- Myrna Loy, *Being and Becoming*, Primus/Donald I. Fine, Inc. New York, 1988 (p.139)

In popular culture

Literature

- In 1979, Manuel Puig published the fantasy novel *Pubis Angelical (en)*, inspired by the story of Lamarr (wife of a major European arms dealer and film star), in which he reduces women to pure sexual fantasy.
- Géraldine Beigbeder published her first novel in 2007, a *road-movie* in search of *sponsors in* post-Communist Eastern Europe for a feature film about Hedy Lamarr, the legendary anti-Nazi star of the 1930s.
- *Anarquia* (2004), a novel by Brad Linaweaver and J. Kent Hastings, presents an alternative history of the Spanish Civil War from 1936 to 1939: artists, émigré writers, reporters, philosophers, political activists (Hedy Lamarr, Wernher von Braun, Ernest Hemingway, George Orwell, John Dos Passos, Ayn Rand, G. K. Chesterton...) carry the hopes of the world on their shoulders.
- A banned biography of Marlon Brando describes Hedy Lamarr as the "queen of orgasms" over several pages, with salacious dialogue between the actor and her (Darwin Porter, *Brando Unzipped*, 2006).

- In 2008, Devra Z. Hill published a book, *What Almost Happened to Hedy Lamarr*, described as a "fictionalized biography" by Ruth Barton, in which the author describes the star's Sapphic sexual relations and her affair with Hitler (whose gifts Hedy Lamarr shows off).

Cinema

- Walt Disney's fictional Snow White character is said to have been inspired by Hedy Lamarr's physique ("jet-black hair, porcelain complexion and azure eyes" according to articles published as of 2018).
- Director Ridley Scott drew inspiration from Lamarr to design the hieratically beautiful face of the "replicant" Rachel in Blade Runner. Rachel in *Blade Runner,* 1982.
- Ingmar Bergman wrote *Un été avec Monika* (1952) for Harriet Andersson, and drew inspiration from Hedy in *Extase* (filmed twenty years earlier) for the nude scene, one of the first in post-war Europe.
- In 1974, Mel Brooks used his name accompanied by the sound of a fart in *The Sheriff is in Jail*. H. Lamarr sues him.
- In 2017, Alexandra Dean directed the film *Hedy Lamarr: From Extase to Wifi*, revealing in

particular her love life as well as her talents as an inventor during the Second World War.

- In 2019, London's National Portrait Gallery is acquiring an original Italian poster by Luigi Martinati (it) for Jean Negulesco's film *Les Conspirateurs* (1944), showing her drawn in profile; "her image reflects the appeal that led her to be called 'the most beautiful woman in the world'".

Television

- In 2017, Hedy Lamarr, played by actress Celia Massingham, was a main character in an episode of the *DC* series *Legends of Tomorrow* (season 3, episode *The Beautiful Helen of Troy*). *Screenrant* classifies this appearance by Hedy Lamarr as the most interesting of all the appearances of historical figures in this series.
- In the animated series *Hey Arnold!* Hedy Lamarr is mentioned in episode 8 of season 2, entitled *Brutus Caesar*. Arnold's grandfather presents a photo of Hedy Lamarr to a journalist. Furthermore, at the end of this episode, the same character refers to Hedy Lamarr's many marriages, saying he's going to marry her.
- In 2018, she appeared in the series *Timeless* (season 2, episode 3, *Hollywoodland*), played by

Alyssa Sutherland in the company of her pianist
friend George Antheil.

Comic strips

- Hedy Lamarr's features were inspired by those of
  Catwoman, the comic strip character created by
  Bob Kane.
- She is the main heroine in a *one-shot* in author
  Michel Schetter's *Yin-Yang* collection, entitled *Les
  Lettres de Pearl*.
- She appears in Pénélope Bagieu's French comic
  strip dedicated to the striking stories of strong
  women *Culottées 2*, released in 2017.

Video game

- Dr. Isaac Kleiner, a fictional character featured in
  the video game *Half-Life 2*, notably nicknamed his
  tame head crab "Lamarr". He sometimes calls her
  "Hedy".

Military

- "Tondelayo" is the name given by Lieutenant
  Ralph Wallace's crew to a North American B-25
  Mitchell bomber, one of America's most famous
  warplanes, named after Hedy Lamarr's character
  in the film *Tondelayo* (*White Cargo*, 1942), and
  her character Black Venus in the film *Extase*
  (1933).
- *The Ruptured Duck*, the nickname of the
  prestigious military medal *The Honorable*

Discharge Lapel Pin, is attributed to Hedy Lamarr who, flying to escape Friedrich Mandl (who wanted to assassinate her because everyone had discovered that she was the author of the military inventions he had claimed for himself), compared her terrible flight to a "*segeltuch gebrochen*" (*broken bird),* but this was translated as "*ruptured duck*". The expression was taken up by the employees of the factory that manufactured the *Duck* to commemorate Lamarr's heroic flight.

Sciences
- In 1998, the Ars Electronica festival paid tribute to the star H. Lamarr and the inventor.
- Since 2005, German-speaking countries have celebrated "Inventors' Day" every November 9, the anniversary of his birth.

Internet
- In 2015, on her birthday, the Google website displayed a doodle dedicated to Hedy Lamarr on its homepage.
- On the Internet, Hedy Lamarr has generated a real trade, with "Hedy Lamarr dresses" and tee shirts featuring the quote "The secret of life is to try everything".

Music

- In 2001, German artist Michaela Melián paid tribute to both Hedy with her creation *Life as a Woman, Hedy Lamarr.*
- In 2010, *Ballet Mécanique: A Spread-Spectrum Ecstasy was performed* at the Hegsbourg Center Auditorium of the Université de Notre-Dame-du-Lac, featuring a reading of John Matthias's poem *Automystifstical Plaice*, taken from his book *Working Progress* and inspired by Hedy Lamarr's life, her marriage to Mandl and her collaboration with Antheil.
- In 2015, Thézame Barrême (lyrics and vocals) and Abdul Jaba (piano) created a musical duo in Arles called "hədylamarr" (written with a tumbled e).
- In 2022, Jeff Beck and Johnny Depp dedicated one of the songs on their collaborative album *18 to* her, entitled *This Is A Song For Miss Hedy Lamarr*.

Personality

- Dita von Teese confesses her fascination for 1940s actresses such as Hedy Lamarr and Rita Hayworth, as does fashion designer Valentino, another admirer of yesterday's star.

Other books by United Library

https://campsite.bio/unitedlibrary

Printed in the USA
CPSIA information can be obtained
at www.ICGtesting.com
CBHW070511060724
11224CB00008B/466

9 789464 902624